W9-BZC-089

17.99

REPTILES & AMPHIBIANS

FROGS, TOADS, & SALAMANDERS

Chris McNab

GARETH**STEVENS**

GS

PUBLISHING

A Member of the WRC Media Family of Companies

Please visit our web site at: **www.garethstevens.com**
For a free color catalog describing Gareth Stevens Publishing's
list of high-quality books and multimedia programs,
call 1-800-542-2595 (USA) or 1-800-387-3178 (Canada).
Gareth Stevens Publishing's fax: (414) 332-3567.

Library of Congress Cataloging-in-Publication Data

McNab, Chris.
 Frogs, toads, & salamanders / Chris McNab. — North American ed.
  p. cm. — (Nature's monsters: Reptiles & amphibians)
 Includes bibliographical references and index.
 ISBN 0-8368-6172-8 (lib. bdg.)
 1. Frogs—Juvenile literature. 2. Toads—Juvenile literature.
 3. Salamanders—Juvenile literature. I. Title: Frogs, toads, and salamanders.
 II. Title. III. Series.
 QL668.E2M36 2006
 597.8—dc22   2005054341

This North American edition first published in 2006 by
Gareth Stevens Publishing
A Member of the WRC Media Family of Companies
330 West Olive Street, Suite 100
Milwaukee, WI 53212 USA

Original edition and illustrations copyright © 2006 by International Masters Publishers AB.
Produced by Amber Books Ltd., Bradley's Close, 74–77 White Lion Street, London N1 9PF, U.K.

Project editor: Michael Spilling
Design: Joe Conneally

Gareth Stevens editorial direction: Valerie J. Weber
Gareth Stevens art direction: Tammy West
Gareth Stevens production: Jessica Morris

Printed in the United States of America

1 2 3 4 5 6 7 8 9 10 09 08 07 06

Contents

Continents of the World

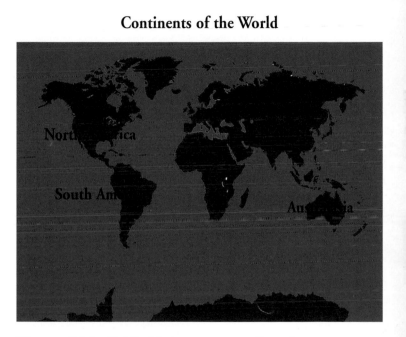

The world is divided into seven continents — North America, South America, Europe, Africa, Asia, Australasia, and Antarctica. In this book, the area where each animal lives is shown in red, while all land is shown in green.

Words that appear in the glossary are printed in **boldface** type the first time they occur in the text.

Axolotl

The axolotl's eyes are very small and have no eyelids.

The axolotl (AK-suh-lah-tul) uses its **gills** to take **oxygen** from the water. The axolotl needs oxygen to survive.

The axolotl feels the movements of other animals in the water through its skin.

The axolotl's feet have webbed toes. It uses them like paddles.

In their natural environment, axolotls remain infants for their entire lives, never growing up to be adult animals.

▶**1** If an axolotl is allowed to grow to become an adult, its body changes. It loses its gills and tail fin, it grows eyelids, and its skin becomes thicker.

If an axolotl loses one of its limbs, it will grow a completely new one. This ability is useful because in **captivity**, axolotls often bite off each other's toes and feet.

▶**2** The reason that axolotls do not grow into fully formed adults may be because they live in very cold water. Cold water can stop their growth **hormones** from working well.

Where in the World

In the wild, axolotls live only in Lake Xochimilco, high in the mountains of Mexico. Most axolotls, however, are now kept in captivity by scientists or as pets.

▶**3** Because axolotls have feet and legs, they can walk under the water as well as swim.

Giant Salamander

Rows of tiny sharp teeth help the giant salamander trap its **prey** in its mouth.

The giant salamander uses its powerful tail to swim quickly through the water.

Its skin is slack, slimy, and smooth all over, except on its head.

Giant salamanders come in many different colors, from a greyish pink to black.

Giant salamanders can seem slow in the water, especially when it is daytime. At night, however, they become fast hunters; no fish swimming near them is safe.

The giant salamander is the world's largest **amphibian**. The largest ever found was a Chinese giant salamander that was 6 feet (1.8 meters) long. Most are usually 3 feet (1 m) long.

A giant salamander lurks at the bottom of a stream. It uses the dark shadow of an overhanging rock to hide itself from passing fish. Suddenly a fish swims a few inches away from its hiding place.

2 The salamander shoots out. It grabs the fish in its jaws. Although the fish is slippery, the salamander's sharp teeth grip it firmly for eating.

Where in the World

Giant salamanders inhabit mountainous streams and rivers. They are mainly found in China and in Japan, although a **species** also lives on the Pacific coast of North America.

Fire-Bellied Toad

Its skin oozes a mildly poisonous slime when the toad feels threatened.

The eyes of the fire-bellied toad are set high on its head so it can see all around.

The fire-bellied toad's **webbed** feet are good for swimming and digging down into mud.

The fire-bellied toad has a bright red pattern on its belly to warn **predators** away.

A fire-bellied toad has a special way of scaring off predators. With its **double-jointed** limbs it takes the "canoe position," showing off its brightly colored belly and legs and oozing poison.

The male fire-bellied toad can croak while it is breathing in. This ability is unusual because most frogs and toads can only croak when they are breathing out.

◀ 1 When threatened, the toad lifts up its head and tail and puts its legs on the top of its body. It displays its bright red back legs and its colorful red-and-black belly. In animals, bright colors often mean something is poisonous.

Where in the World

There are six types of fire-bellied toads. They live in many parts of Europe and in China in Asia. They are mostly found in shallow lakes or ponds.

▶ 2 Special **glands** in the toad's skin make a milky liquid. This liquid is poisonous.

Marine Toad

Its **parotid glands** make a strong milky poison, which is dangerous even to large animals and humans.

Powerful legs help the toad crawl quickly when chasing mice, snakes, and other frogs.

The marine toad can grip a wriggling snake with its front feet.

The marine toad has strong jaws for holding and swallowing its prey.

10

The marine toad is the world's biggest toad. Its size can make it look like a big meal for predators. Trying to eat one, however, can be deadly.

▶1 A Gould's monitor lizard in Australia gets ready to attack a marine toad. The toad puffs up its body, trying to make itself look bigger and stronger.

The marine toad was brought to Australia to eat pests on sugarcane **plantations**. People started calling it the cane toad. The toad itself has become a pest, however, because no other animal can eat this poisonous creature.

◀2 The monitor is not scared off. It leaps forward and clamps its bone-crushing jaws around the toad. The toad releases a foul-tasting **venom** into the monitor's mouth.

◀3 The monitor releases the toad and starts to shake as the poison works through its body. In minutes, it is dead.

Where in the World?

The marine toad lives in South and Central America and in the southern United States. It was introduced into Australia in 1935.

Ornate Horned Frog

The frog's skin colors help it blend in with leaves on a forest floor.

The ornate horned frog is one of the largest in the world. It often weighs up to 1 pound (500 grams).

The ornate horned frog's mouth is almost as wide as its large head.

The frog uses its powerful legs for jumping and swimming.

The ornate horned frog is a big amphibian, growing up to 6 inches (15 centimeters) in length. It will try to eat anything, even birds.

1 Without moving, the frog waits on the forest floor. A bird called a flycatcher lands in front of it, looking for insects.

2 The flycatcher does not see the danger. The frog pounces and grabs the bird in its huge mouth.

3 The frog now eats the whole bird. Its meal is so large that the bird's legs poke out of the frog's mouth.

Young ornate horned frogs use a special trick to catch prey. They sometimes waggle their toes. This movement attracts prey who think the toes are tasty insects. When the prey gets close, the frog grabs it.

The ornate horned frog is found in Brazil, Uruguay, Paraguay, and Argentina. It lives mainly in the **rain forests**, although some frogs live in **pampas grass** prairies.

Poison Dart Frog

The poison dart frog has large eyes to help it see in the gloomy jungle.

Poison dart frogs can have blue, green, red, or yellow skin. Their skin is often brightly patterned with spots and stripes. In nature, bright colors mean danger.

The skin leaks **mucus** and a milky white deadly poison·from special glands.

The frog has suckers on its toes so it can climb the highest trees.

Human hunters in the rain forests of South America use the **toxins** of the poison dart frog on their arrows and **blowpipe** darts. The Choco Indians of Colombia have a cruel way of getting the poison out of the frog.

▶ **1** The Indian pins the frog to the ground with a stick. He carefully holds the frog in a leaf and traps it in the end of a split cane. He holds the frog over a fire.

Just a small amount of poison from the poison dart frog on the skin could easily kill a human being. The poison from one poison dart frog can be enough to kill more than a thousand people!

◀ **2** The frog burns over the fire, and its poison bubbles out of its skin. In the heat, the toxin becomes thick like glue.

▲ **3** The Indian rubs the point of his darts in the poison. Each dart has enough poison to kill a large monkey.

Poison dart frogs are found in the humid tropical rain forests of Central and South America. No one knows how many species there are, and new ones are found every year.

Budgett's Frog

The frog's eyes bulge outward, and it can see well both in the daytime and at night.

The frog's skin is covered with mucus to stop it from losing moisture.

Its back legs are very powerful; they are designed for pushing through mud.

Its bottom jaw has two points that look like teeth. The frog uses these points for biting.

A Budgett's frog is always hunting for food. It will try to eat almost any other animal it can fit into its huge mouth.

1 Two Budgett's frogs meet each other while looking for food. Their bodies swell up, and their mouths open as they get ready to fight.

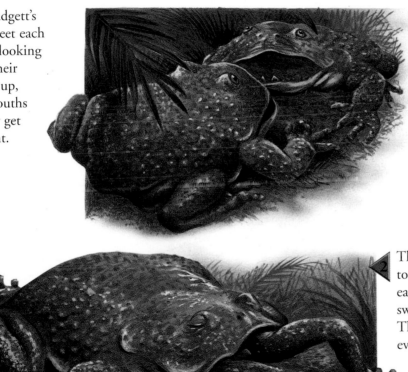

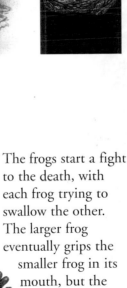

When Budgett's frogs are used for **breeding** in zoos, the male and female frog must be separated right after **mating**. Otherwise they might try to eat each other.

2 The frogs start a fight to the death, with each frog trying to swallow the other. The larger frog eventually grips the smaller frog in its mouth, but the meal is too big to swallow. The larger frog chokes. Both frogs die.

Where in the World

The Budgett's frog **inhabits** inland areas of Paraguay and Argentina in South America. It lives in small ponds and shallow pools. The frog wraps itself in wet mud during hot weather.

Mantella Frog

Glands in the frog's skin produce moisture and also dangerous poisons.

The mantella (man-TELL-ah) frog has special toe pads to help it climb up trees.

The mantella frog's large eyes see well in the gloomy forests.

It uses the skin around its throat to make different sounds or calls.

Frogs often look tasty to predators. The poisonous skin of the mantella frog, however, means that predators are in danger themselves if they try to eat one.

1 A snake hunting for insects spots a mantella frog on the forest floor. It decides that the frog will make an easy meal.

2 The snake creeps closer, then opens its mouth and snaps its jaws shut on the frog. The frog is almost inside the snake's mouth.

3 Quickly, the mantella frog pumps out toxins from its skin. The snake's mouth feels like it is burning, and it fills with a very bad taste. The snake spits out the frog, and the frog crawls away unhurt.

The poisons in the mantella frogs' skin are extremely **toxic**. If they enter a person's body through a cut, the person will die. Some hunters in Africa use frog poisons on the tips of their arrows and blowpipe darts.

Mantella frogs live in the rain forests on the island of Madagascar. The island is off the eastern coast of Africa. Many species live here that are not found anywhere else.

Malaysian Horned Toad

The toad's three "horns" are made of skin. They confuse predators because most toads do not have these shapes.

The horned toad has powerful eyes that can see well in the dark.

The toad's skin pattern looks like fallen leaves. It can change color to **camouflage** itself.

The male horned toad uses the skin around its throat to make calls to attract female horned toads.

Female Malaysian horned toads are bigger than the males. Although horned toads eat insects, mice, and lizards, the female will sometimes even eat a male.

When it is threatened, the horned toad sucks in air through its mouth to make itself look bigger. This trick may scare off any predators.

A female horned toad sits still and silent on the jungle floor. She hears an animal moving toward her through the **undergrowth**.

She spots a small male horned toad approaching. When it is close enough, she leaps forward and grabs it by the back leg.

The horned toad has a very powerful mouth, and the unlucky male cannot escape. The female slowly swallows him whole. She rolls back her eyes to help force the big mouthful down her throat.

The horned toad lives in the rain forests of Southeast Asia, hiding among the plants. The rain forests have a damp climate that keeps the toad moist.

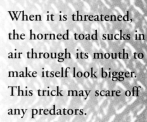

Pipa Toad

The female pipa (PEE-pah) toad has special pits in its back where its young can grow.

The toad can easily swallow large prey with its big mouth.

The pipa toad has a flat body. It can squash itself into the ground to hide from predators.

Its nostrils can poke out of the water to breathe while the toad stays hidden beneath the surface.

The pipa toad will wait many hours to pounce on its prey. Eyes are almost useless in deep muddy water, but the pipa toad's extralong fingers help it feel for its prey.

1 The pipa toad hides on the bottom of a river. Its color and shape make it look the same as the leaves around it. A fish swims close by.

The pipa toad spends much of its time under water, but it still needs to breathe. About every half hour, it swims to the surface to take a gulp of air.

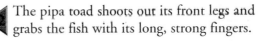

2 The pipa toad shoots out its front legs and grabs the fish with its long, strong fingers.

Where in the World

The pipa toad inhabits **tropical** parts of South and Central America. It likes rivers, ponds, and streams with plenty of plants in and near the water.

3 The toad uses its fingers to draw the fish into its mouth. The toad swallows the fish whole.

Paradoxical Frog

As **tadpoles, paradoxical** (per-uh-DAHK-sih-kul) frogs grow up to 10 inches (25 cm) long.

Its front legs have long toes to help the frog hold its prey.

Its back toes are webbed to help it swim well.

The frog's nose is on top of its head. The animal can float just beneath the surface of the water but still breathe.

Paradoxical frogs breed like most other frogs. When the eggs develop, however, they grow into the world's biggest tadpoles.

The male and female paradoxical toads make **spawn** together. The eggs float on the surface of the water and develop into tadpoles.

The tadpoles feed all the time. They grow to be four times bigger than the adult frog, reaching up to 10 inches (25 cm) in length.

The tadpole's tail disappears, and the frog grows a different mouth and legs. The adult frog is only about 1 to 3 inches (2.5 to 7.5 cm) long.

Paradoxical frogs may not look good to eat, but some people in South America do hunt them for food. They catch them in nets and then cook and eat them.

The paradoxical frog lives in the tropical parts of South America. It likes the rain forest or any place that is damp and has lots of rain.

African Bullfrog

The African bullfrog can inflate its body to twice its normal size to scare its enemies.

A bony bump grows on the bullfrog's foot. It uses this bump to dig into soil.

The bullfrog grabs its prey with its front hands or licks up insects with its sticky tongue.

A bullfrog can open its mouth so wide it can eat a whole rat.

Frogs need to remain moist at all times, or they will die. In the dry African climates the African bullfrog has a sure way to survive the dry season.

A female bullfrog can lay an incredible four thousand eggs at one time. Other animals will eat most of them, but enough will survive to hatch into new frogs.

The bullfrog digs down into the African soil, using its powerful back legs to push the dirt behind it. It goes deeper and deeper under ground until it is cool and protected from the sun.

The bullfrog makes a **cocoon** around itself using flakes of skin held together with mucus. The cocoon keeps moisture in and stops the frog from drying out. Bullfrogs can stay like this for several months, returning to the surface only when the rains come.

Where in the World?

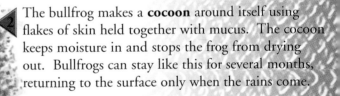

The African bullfrog lives in **savannas** and deserts in Africa. It likes to be near water, so it is often found in pools or living along riverbanks.

Crested Newt

Adult male crested newts grow large crests along their backs to attract females.

Its belly is brightly colored to warn predators about the newt's horrible taste.

Long, thin toes help the newt wrap its eggs in leaves to hide them from other animals.

Special glands in the newt's skin ooze a fluid that tastes bad to predators.

Adult crested newts are hungry creatures. They eat worms, water snails, insect **larvae**, spawn, and tadpoles.

1 A large adult crested newt is hiding in weeds at the bottom of a pond. Suddenly a smaller crested newt swims close by.

2 The larger newt jumps out and grabs the smaller animal in its mouth. It shakes its prey quickly until it stops struggling.

The larger newt swallows its prey whole. It takes the head into its mouth first so the legs fold back and **3** slip down its throat easily.

Even as adults, crested newts continue to grow. As they become bigger they have to shed their old skin. Newts eat this old skin as a tasty meal.

The crested newt is found in much of northern and central Europe. It lives in ponds and rivers and near water.

Glossary

amphibian — an animal that lives entirely in water as an infant, breathing through its gills. When it has grown into an adult, it can move onto land and breathe using lungs.

blowpipe — a hollow tube that fires a dart when a person blows hard at one end of the tube

breeding — when two animals are brought together to make babies

camouflage — to hide or disguise

captivity — held in a cage or kept from escaping

cocoon — a pouch or case that helps protect an animal

double-jointed — describes joints of an animal's limbs that will bend in opposite directions

gills — the parts of an animal used for breathing under water

glands — parts of the body that make special chemicals needed for the body to work properly

hormones — chemicals in the bodies of animals that help them grow and develop

inhabits — lives in

larvae —the early form of animals such as frogs and insects, just after they have hatched from their eggs

mating — the act of breeding

mucus — a thick, jellylike liquid made by an animal to protect its body

oxygen — a gas that makes up about 20 percent of the air animals breathe. It is also present in water.

pampas grass — a tall grass that grows in large, dense clumps on the plains (pampas) of South America

paradoxical — something that seems to be the opposite of what it actually is

parotid glands — warty poisonous glands found on the head and back of some frogs and salamanders

plantations — huge farms planted in just a few crops

predators — animals that hunt other animals for food

prey — an animal hunted for food

rain forests — thick forests, often in tropical regions, where a lot of rain falls

savannas — open grassland, scattered with bushes and trees

spawn — the eggs of many animals that live in water

species — a group of living things of the same family or type

tadpoles — very young frogs or toads; they have gills, long tail fins, and no legs

toxic — poisonous

toxins — poisons made by an animal or plant

tropical — referring to the warmest regions of the world, with lush plant life and lots of rain

undergrowth — low-growing plants and shrubs

venom — a poison made by an animal

webbed — covered in a thin layer of skin

For More Information

Books

Amazing Amphibians. Watts Library: Animals (series). Sara Swan Miller (Franklin Watts)

Frogs and Toads. The Secret World of (series). Jill Bailey (Raintree)

Frogs and Toads: The Leggy Leapers. Animals in Order (series). Sara Swan Miller (Franklin Watts)

Frogs, Toads, and Turtles. Take-along Guide (series). Diane. L. Burns (Northwood Press)

Investigate Frogs and Toads. Investigate (series). Gary Fleming and Dr. David Kirshner (Whitecap Books)

Salamanders: Secret, Silent Lives. Animals in Order (series). Sara Swan Miller (Franklin Watts)

The Amazing Book of Reptile and Amphibian Records: The Largest, the Fastest, the Most Poisonous, and Many More! Animal Records (series). Samuel G. Woods (Blackbirch Press)

Toads. Animal Kingdom (series). Julie Murray (ABDO Books)

Web Sites

All About Frogs
allaboutfrogs.org/frogland.shtml

All About Frogs for Kids and Teachers
www.kiddyhouse.com/Themes/frogs/frogs.html

Jumping Into Frogs and Toads
projects.edtech.sandi.net/lvelem/frogsandtoads

Rocky Mountain National Wildlife Refuge
rockymountainarsenal.fws.gov/wildlife/ reptilesAmphibians/amphibians.htm

Smithsonian National Zoological Park: Reptiles & Amphibians
nationalzoo.si.edu/Animals/ReptilesAmphibians

Index